Original title:
Life Lessons From the Ice Cream Cart

Copyright © 2025 Creative Arts Management OÜ
All rights reserved.

Author: Helena Marchant
ISBN HARDBACK: 978-1-80566-136-8
ISBN PAPERBACK: 978-1-80566-431-4

Flavors of Friendship

In a world of cones and scoops,
We share our laughs, our silly loops.
A flavor here, a sprinkle there,
With friends, we mix without a care.

Chocolate chips and vanilla dreams,
We chase our hopes like melting creams.
With every bite, we taste the fun,
Together we shine, two hearts as one.

When life gets tough, just grab a cone,
A scoop of joy, you're never alone.
Friends add sprinkles, a burst of cheer,
Together we make the worries disappear.

So here's to flavors of every kind,
In our shared bowl, sweet memories unwind.
A scoop of laughter, a dash of sweet strife,
We savor each moment, that's friendship in life.

Sprinkled Life Lessons

Chocolate rivers, vanilla skies,
In this sundae, the secret lies.
Add a cherry, make it bright,
Sprinkle joy, it feels just right.

Sometimes it drips, don't let it stain,
Laughter echoes through the pain.
A cone can crumble, but we won't fret,
It's messy fun, no need to sweat.

Scoop by scoop, we learn to share,
Extra toppings show we care.
We mix our flavors, swirl them tight,
Together we bloom in pure delight.

So let's dig in, embrace the mess,
With giggles and grins, we are truly blessed.
Life's a sundae, we make it divine,
With sprinkles of joy, our hearts intertwine.

A Scoop of Gratitude

A cart rolls by, what a sight,
Colors swirl, sunny and bright.
With every cone, a smile appears,
Let's scoop away our little fears.

Flavors dance like silly tunes,
Chocolate, vanilla, under the moons.
A sprinkles shower makes you grin,
Thankful for each scoop within.

The Joy of Simple Pleasures

An ice cream truck, a joyful sound,
Chasing it down, joy's finally found.
A simple cone can lift the day,
Melting troubles all away.

Laughter shared with friends nearby,
Stories drizzled like raspberry pie.
Sticky fingers, happy hearts,
In this moment, trouble departs.

Tasting the Rainbow

Red, green, and blue, what a surprise,
Tasting the rainbow in every bite.
Strawberry giggles, minty laughs,
Flavorful joy in cheerful drafts.

Life's a mix, just like the scoop,
Swirls of happiness, joyful loop.
Count the flavors, don't be shy,
Life's best moments, passing by.

Creamy Dreams

In a waffle cone, dreams reside,
Scoop them up, let's enjoy the ride.
With each lick, let worries cease,
In ice cream land, we find our peace.

Chasing drips with eager hands,
Laughter lingers, sweet ribbons expand.
Savoring every chilly delight,
Creamy dreams keep spirits bright.

Lessons

Sometimes life drips from the cone,
Embrace the mess, you're not alone.
Scoops may wobble, that's the thrill,
Find joy in flavors, perfect still.

Like ice cream, friends come and go,
But the sweet memories, let them flow.
So grab a scoop, life's not so tough,
With laughter, a sprinkle is enough.

Melodies from the Parlor

The vendor's bell sings sweet and bright,
Scoops can turn wrongs into right.
Chasing cones through heat and strife,
A sprinkles' joy can spice up life.

Waffle cups on sunny days,
Melted whims in silly ways.
A hint of fudge, a cherry on top,
With each lick, the laughter won't stop.

Candied Days and Icy Nights

When sundae dreams come floating by,
A scoop of risk beneath the sky.
Chocolate chips and gummy bears,
Keep your worries, share the flares.

At twilight, watch the sprinkles gleam,
Life's sweeter than it might seem.
With every bite, we dance and whirl,
Tasting joy in every swirl.

Flavorful Paths We Take

Each flavor tells a quirky tale,
Minty fresh or a chocolate sail.
Some stumble on a melting cone,
But taste is best when you've outgrown.

With every scoop, a chance to cheer,
Strawberry laughs, no room for fear.
Double dip in laughter's game,
Life's a cone; you'll never blame.

Savoring Each Drip

As cream drips down my eager hand,
I giggle at this tasty brand.
In messy joy, the lessons flow,
Take a bite and let it show.

A flake of joy can save the day,
Unexpected moments in the fray.
So here's to cones and sticky smiles,
We'll savor sweet for miles and miles.

A Cone at Twilight

At the twilight, cones shimmer,
Flavors dance, a sweet glimmer.
Chocolate drips and laughter spills,
Chasing dreams with sundae thrills.

Kids chase pigeons, dogs chase tails,
Whipped cream sails on candy trails.
Life's a swirl, a merry go,
Taste it all, don't take it slow.

Ribbons of Cream and Dreams

Ribbons swirl, a whimsy blend,
Every scoop, a sugar friend.
Minty whispers in the air,
Giggles hidden everywhere.

Cherry tops on sunny days,
Melting worries in sweet ways.
With each taste, the world feels light,
Swirl that cone, it's a delight.

Sprinkles of Joy

Sprinkles rain down, oh what fun,
Candy colors in the sun.
Who knew joy could taste so sweet?
Every lick's a special treat.

In a cup or sugar cone,
Every flavor feels like home.
So grab a scoop, don't hesitate,
Laugh a little, it's first-rate!

Chilling Truths Beneath the Surface

Underneath that creamy dome,
Chilling truths beneath the foam.
Squirrels snack on crumbs around,
As we spin in joy unbound.

Every scoop's a chance to see,
Life's a frosty mystery.
Mix the flavors, stack them high,
Taste the fun as days go by.

The Joy of Confectionary Curiosity

In colors bright, they call to me,
A scoop of dreams, oh what a spree!
With sprinkles dancing, joy does burst,
I wonder which one will quench my thirst?

The choices roll, a sugary race,
Like life itself, it's a merry chase.
Should I go chocolate, the classic scoop?
Or daring mango, a fruity loop?

Learning in the Lick

A lollipop here, a cone with taste,
Each little lick, no second to waste.
If it melts too fast, don't wear a frown,
Just grab a spoon, and dig right down!

In sticky hands, mistakes are sweet,
The mess we make just can't be beat.
For in each flavor, there's joy to find,
Embrace the drip, don't lag behind!

Pleasure in the Pints

A tub of joy just calls my name,
Each creamy bite sets taste buds aflame.
With every scoop, there's wisdom to seek,
Sometimes the best lays hidden, unique.

With friends around, we share our finds,
In every pint, our laughter binds.
The cherry on top, a symbol, you see,
Together we've built our own jubilee!

A Cart Full of Chances

A street-side cart, oh what a sight,
With flavors swirling, pure delight!
I tiptoe close, what will I choose?
Each little scoop is a win or lose.

Minty fresh or berry bold,
The tales they tell, worth their weight in gold.
So take a chance, don't hesitate,
For every cone can unlock your fate!

Sugar and Spice Reflections

A scoop of joy, a sprinkle bright,
Melting worries, pure delight.
Each cone a twist of fate's own hand,
Life's best bites are simply unplanned.

Licking troubles, sweet and cold,
Tasty stories waiting to be told.
Sugar rush on a sunny day,
Chasing shadows far away.

The colorful cart rolls down the lane,
With laughter, lessons, and a touch of rain.
In every flavor, a hint of cheer,
Life tastes better when friends are near.

Flavors of Forgiveness

Minty moments, fresh and clean,
Melting grudges, what a scene!
A cherry on top for every fight,
Who knew sweet could feel so right?

Sprinkles added make it grand,
Forgive and taste, just take my hand.
Pistachio peace, a scoop of grace,
Savoring smiles in this funny race.

Chocolate drips bring laughter near,
Every bite, a wholesome cheer.
Life's too scrumptious to hold a grudge,
In this cart of joy, we always judge.

Sweet Lessons Wrapped in Waffle

Waffle cones with pockets deep,
Holding secrets we can keep.
A scoop of wisdom, creamy and light,
Crunchy edges make it right.

Each flavor teaches, oh so sweet,
In every bite, a special treat.
Sprinkled woes, whipped cream smiles,
Navigating life's funny miles.

In the drip of hot fudge's embrace,
We find joy in the messy space.
So grab a cone, take a chance,
In this dance of sweet romance.

A Taste of Time

Time's a sundae, layered high,
Scoops of moments as they fly.
Caramel drizzle, syrupy tales,
In every bite, adventure sails.

Savor each scoop, don't rush the day,
A cone of wisdom in the fray.
Sometimes it drips, and that's just fine,
Laughter sweetens the aged wine.

Frosty whispers of days gone by,
Teach us to laugh, teach us to sigh.
Chill out, my friend, enjoy the ride,
Seek the flavors that help you glide.

Temporary Melodies

A scoop of joy in sunny days,
Sprinkles dance in playful ways.
Melodies swirl, flavors collide,
Life's little treats, take them in stride.

With each cone, a giggle erupts,
Chasing dreams and syrupy cups.
Laughter melts in warm summer air,
Lessons soft serve, sweet and rare.

Taste Life's Variety

Chocolate, vanilla, or minty green,
Each flavor a tale, unseen.
Life's a cone, stack it up high,
Don't skip the nuts; give them a try.

Sometimes it's messy, a drip and a fall,
But oh how we savor the sweet, after all.
With every lick, a new chance to cheer,
Taste the world, it's all waiting here.

Cold Comforts

An ice cream truck rolls down the lane,
Bringing smiles like a warm summer rain.
Cones in hand, we share our delight,
Cold comforts shining in the twilight.

In sticky fingers and chocolate stains,
We find joy amidst the mundane pains.
A scoop of laughter, a dash of fun,
Forget the worries, go on, run!

Drips of Resilience

When flavors fall and cones go snap,
Laughter rises from every mishap.
A drippy mess, yet oh so sweet,
Each spill's a bounce, not a defeat.

Life's an ice cream, with ups and downs,
Savor the taste, wear sticky crowns.
For every drop, a lesson to learn,
Embrace the chaos, let the ice cream churn.

The Scoop on Growing Up

A scoop of joy, a dollop of fear,
Sprinkles of dreams, and a twist of cheer.
Melting fast in the sun's warm light,
Growing up's messy, but oh what a sight!

With every flavor, we learn to embrace,
The sticky moments we can't quite replace.
Chocolate fudge on your nose, oh dear!
Laughter erupts as we taste the year!

Frosty Insights in a Waffle Cone

A waffle cone is never too plain,
Add a scoop of hopes, joy, and a grain.
Life crumbles at times, let's admit,
But add some sprinkles, and it'll be a hit!

When flavors collide, and choices are made,
Don't panic, my friend, enjoy the parade!
Embrace the melting, the drips, and the fun,
For frosty insights may just weigh a ton!

A Taste of Patience

Waiting in line for a sweet little treat,
Patience is key, don't hurry your feat.
As ice cream softens, so do our hearts,
Savor each moment, it's where joy starts.

Tip your cone carefully, avoid the spill,
Life's about balance, and finding your thrill.
A bite of good humor, a sprinkle of glee,
In the scoop of the day, find your jubilee!

Chocolate Drizzles and Life's Twists

Life's like a sundae with twists that surprise,
Chocolate drizzles like truth in disguise.
When things get tough, and you start to scowl,
Remember the joy in a playful growl.

Nuts may fall out, and the cherry might roll,
But laughter remains, it's the heart of the whole.
So grab your cone, and let worries unwind,
For chocolate drizzles are one of a kind!

Sweet Cones of Experience

A scoop of joy in every cone,
Watch out for the drip, it's overgrown!
Life's a sundae, a mix so wild,
Often it feels like a messy child.

In choosing flavors, don't just stick,
Try something daring, go for the kick!
Chocolate's safe, but where's the thrill?
Taste the rainbow, embrace the chill!

Flavors of Understanding

Mint chocolate chip, a favorite for sure,
But bubblegum's there, if you want something pure!
Life's a menu, a vast array,
Try each flavor, come what may.

Every scoop teaches something new,
Blueberry dreams or vanilla too.
With each bite, a giggle or sigh,
Sometimes you laugh, sometimes you cry.

Chilled Reflections

Sitting back with a cone in hand,
Like life's surprises, it's all unplanned!
A hint of salt, a dash of sweet,
Sometimes it feels like a messy treat.

Melting faster than you can think,
Grab a napkin, don't miss the pink!
It's all about balance, don't you see?
A smile appears, and that's the key!

Sprinkles of Truth

Life's just like a sprinkle parade,
Too much can ruin the sweet charade!
A little chaos is all in fun,
But too many toppings can weigh a ton.

Share a cone, share a laugh,
Find joy in the silly, not just the half!
With every scoop, embrace the play,
It's all about savoring each day!

Sunshine and Scoops of Hope

Under the sun, the colors swirl,
Children laugh, their dreams unfurl.
A scoop so big, it topples right,
A lesson learned, hold on tight.

Chocolates melt, and sprinkles fly,
Giggles bubble, we can't deny.
With every cone that drips and falls,
We find the joy in sticky brawls.

Flavors clash like wild ideas,
Some make you smile, some bring tears.
Vanilla plain, or berry bold,
Mix them up; that's how we roll!

So grab a spoon and make a mess,
In every scoop, there's happiness.
Beneath the sun, we taste our dreams,
Bittersweet, just like our schemes.

The Cart of Aspirations

At the cart, we stack our hopes,
Waffle cups and golden ropes.
Strawberry dreams and chocolate schemes,
A sprinkle here, a scoop of memes.

The vendor grins, he knows the trick,
Life's like ice cream, it's quick and slick.
Choose your flavors, dare to blend,
With each cone, we twist and bend.

Swirls of joy, the sundae glows,
A funny twist that nobody knows.
When it drips down your brand-new shirt,
Just laugh it off, and don't get hurt.

So when in doubt, go for a scoop,
Join the fun, jump in the loop.
For every cone holds secrets bold,
Our cart of dreams, a sight to behold!

Scoop of Wisdom

A tiny cart rolls down the lane,
Scoops of wisdom, joy, and pain.
A cherry on top of laughter's frown,
In every flavor, quirks abound.

Lemon sorbet for life's sour days,
Chocolate fudge for winding ways.
Pick and choose, don't fear the clash,
Sometimes you win, sometimes you splash.

Like ice cream melts, so does our pride,
Embrace the mess, let laughter slide.
With sticky hands and silly grins,
The sweetest lessons in the spins.

So take a scoop and share a laugh,
In every drip, find your own path.
For in this cart of frozen dreams,
There's wisdom found in silly schemes.

Melting Moments

On summer days, the sunbeats down,
Kids all gather, wearing crowns.
A scoop slips from a butter cone,
Just like dreams can feel alone.

The taste of joy can sometimes spill,
But laughter helps to mend what's ill.
Life's a swirl of flavors bright,
Catch them quick, or face the plight.

A cone that tips can bring surprise,
With every fall, we learn to rise.
Chocolate drips and laughter's dance,
Embrace the mess, give life a chance.

So watch the cart that rolls along,
In every heart, there's room for song.
For melting moments leave their mark,
In every scoop, ignite the spark.

The Sweetness of Now

Summer sun, a joyous blast,
Ice cream smiles, too good to last.
Each cone a treasure, scoop it fast,
In sticky fingers, memories cast.

Swirling flavors, oh what a sight,
Chocolate, vanilla, pure delight.
Sprinkles dance in the warm sunlight,
Licking quickly, taste buds ignite.

Chasing dreams down the melting street,
Strawberry wishes, oh so sweet.
With every lick, life feels complete,
The ice cream cart, a special treat.

An empty cone, a lesson learned,
Savor moments, excitement yearned.
Each scoop a chapter, joy discerned,
In melted puddles, wisdom burned.

Lessons in Every Drip

Watch it wobble, a scoop on top,
One tiny bump, and down it'll flop.
Droplets fall, the sweetest stop,
Life's little spills make hearts hop.

With every dribble, don't you pout,
Taste the mess, it's what it's about.
A playful splash, no need to doubt,
Grab a napkin, let joy sprout.

Every flavor tells a tale,
Minty moments where we prevail.
Cones in hand, we set our sail,
On creamy waves, together we trail.

So when it drips, don't let it go,
Lick it up, let that joy flow.
For every slip, there's room to grow,
In the sticky sweet, life's glow.

Reflecting on Flavors Past

A time of fudge, a cherry cheer,
Nostalgia cloaked in a waffle sphere.
Flavors swirl, as memories near,
Each creamy bite pulls laughter here.

In the mint, a childhood friend,
A scoop shared, where giggles blend.
In every cone, the moments mend,
The taste of joy that will never end.

Staring long at a melting muse,
Coconut dreams, the path we choose.
As time slips by, there's none to lose,
Just flavors swirling, in sweet hues.

So take a scoop from the past's embrace,
Taste the joy, life's funny race.
Each flavor swirls, a warm embrace,
In every cone, we find our place.

Sundae Reflections

Whipped cream towers, a frosty dream,
Nuts and cherries, a sweet regime.
Layers of joy, let laughter beam,
With every spoon, we giggle and scheme.

Chocolate river, a luscious flow,
Sprinkled surprises, watch 'em glow.
In every bite, we learn to grow,
Sundaes served with a side of show.

So when life's ups and downs collide,
Mix it up and enjoy the ride.
For in each cup, our hearts will bide,
Love and laughter, our real guide.

So gather 'round, all friends unite,
Under stars, the world feels right.
With sundaes shared, pure delight,
In every scoop, we spark the night.

Learning to Lick the Cone

If you've ever faced a cone,
Just remember, you're not alone.
It starts off great, a perfect peak,
But then it drips—oh, what a leak!

So, practice quick, with every bite,
Embrace the mess, it feels so right.
A sticky hand, a joyful grin,
Get the napkin, let the fun begin!

Mishaps happen, they're part of the game,
Embrace the drips, don't feel the shame.
For laughter follows each sweet mess,
In sticky moments, you find success!

So take your time, enjoy each scoop,
Life's just like an ice cream loop.
Dig in deep, with all your flair,
And let your laughter fill the air!

The Scoop on Success

A scoop so big, it wobbles high,
Aim for that treat, oh me, oh my!
But careful now, don't lose control,
A topple here could take a toll!

Success sometimes is melting slow,
With flavors mixed, and ebbs and flows.
A swirl of joy and struggles blend,
But laughter makes it all amend!

Remember, friend, each sprinkle bright,
Adds to your path, a pure delight.
So gather round, the gang is here,
For every scoop brings hearts to cheer!

Fudge drips down, but don't you fret,
In every failure, there's no regret.
Just find the joy in every taste,
In the silly moments, there's no waste!

Melting Away Insecurities

Take a scoop, it's all okay,
Insecurities just melt away.
With every cone, embrace the thrill,
Let laughter guide, it's all goodwill.

A scoop of chocolate, rich and bold,
Hides the fears we think we're told.
So take a bite and feel it slide,
Those worries gone, nowhere to hide!

Giggles bubble, ice cream's the cure,
With sprinkles on top, you feel secure.
So laugh aloud, don't be demure,
In every scoop, you find the pure.

As flavors blend, let frowns erase,
In every cone, find your own space.
So lift your head, let spirits soar,
In sweet delight, you'll want for more!

Whimsical Flavors of Existence

Minty green or bubblegum blue,
Life is quirky—it's up to you!
A twist of fate, a cherry on top,
With every flavor, let joy pop!

Lemon zests can make you laugh,
While chocolate's rich, a gentle craft.
From fruity swirls to nutty dreams,
In this great cart, nothing's as it seems!

Dare to mix and try them all,
Life's just a treat at every stall.
So grab a cone, and twirl with glee,
In laughter's scoop, we're truly free!

Embrace the whimsy, taste the fun,
With friends beside, what's done is done.
So share a cone, make memories last,
In every bite, find joys amassed!

The Melodies of Everyday Flavors

The chime of the cart brings a cheer,
As sprinkles dance, like friends who near.
Each scoop a tune, each cone a song,
Life's bright notes, where we belong.

Chocolate chips and minty dreams,
With every lick, the laughter beams.
Rainbow swirls in a summertime breeze,
Moments of joy, aiming to please.

A dribble here, a splash over there,
Messy faces, no room for despair.
Flavors change, but joy stays the same,
In this creamy game, we find our fame.

So grab your cone, don't hesitate,
In the world of sweet, there lies no fate.
As long as we savor this sunny spree,
Every scoop is a lesson in glee.

Life in a Sugar Cone

A cone in hand, the world feels bright,
With every flavor, we light up the night.
Fudge dripping down, chaos in play,
But who needs rules on a sunny day?

Waffles crumble, but smiles won't fade,
The richer the mess, the sweeter the trade.
Cherry on top, life's quirky twist,
Grab a napkin, we can't let it miss!

Stick to your scoop, embrace the mess,
Fearing the drip? Just say yes!
Melted moments, treasures untold,
Life's sugar rush is a sight to behold.

So when you're lost in a swirl of thought,
Remember the joy that ice cream has brought.
With every cone, let's make it clear,
Who needs a plan when happiness is near?

Parables from the Parlor

In the parlor of dreams, flavors collide,
With quirky shakes, and ribbons of pride.
Each sundae, a story, each scoop, a tale,
Where smiles are served with a wink and a scale.

The mint never fades, friendships too sweet,
With each joyful bite, we gather and meet.
Sprinkled wisdom, color it bright,
In the land of ice cream, wrong feels right.

A cherry's plump gloss, deliciously round,
In life's busy rush, it's the sweetness that's found.
Crumbling wafers, sticky hands try,
To hold onto happiness before it runs dry.

So remember this trick, as flavors unfold,
Joy is best captured when shared, not controlled.
With sprightly laughter and ice cream galore,
We learn in the parlor, there's always more.

The Scoop of Experience

A scoop of adventure in a paper cup,
Tasting the world as I slurp it up.
Chocolate chip dough, a curious bite,
Each spoonful serves wisdom, colorful light.

Sticky fingers and giggles all around,
Pineapple whispers of paradise found.
Less is more, as the cone does teach,
Life's sweetest moments are within reach.

An overflowing cone, temptations galore,
Flavors collide, we holler for more.
Sometimes it drips, but that's part of fun,
Experience laughter before it's all done.

So collect your spoons and let's take a ride,
Through sprinkles of joy on this silly slide.
With every lick, let your worries unfurl,
In the scoop of experience, taste the whole world.

The Churning of Time

In the sun, a cart stands bright,
Scoops of joy in every sight.
But hurry up, don't be too late,
Melting dreams just can't wait.

A sprinkle here, a swirl of that,
Life's choices fit in a cone, just pat.
Some days you taste the chocolate bliss,
Others, regret in a sour kiss.

The ice cream drips, just like our plans,
Sticky hands and awkward stands.
Add a cherry on top, a daring feat,
Yet sometimes we taste defeat.

So when in doubt, grab a scoop,
Laugh about it with your troop.
For every flavor brings a lesson clear,
Laugh it off, that's the sweet frontier.

Taffy Tales and Truths

Taffy pulls like life's demands,
Stretch it thick, it slips from hands.
Chewy moments, hard to swallow,
But it's the sweet that we must follow.

In every flavor, truth unveiled,
Caramel dreams, some have failed.
Yet with each bite of honeyed fate,
We find a twist, not just debate.

Fudge so thick, it's hard to spread,
Sometimes we joke before we tread.
Wrap it up in laughter bright,
Or it may never feel quite right.

So cherish the taffy, chew it slow,
Life's glad moments come and go.
With laughs and bonds, we stick together,
Sweet like candy, no matter the weather.

Swirls of Serenity

A cone of calm on busy streets,
Swirls of joy, and laughter meets.
Take a scoop, let worries freeze,
In every bite, find inner peace.

Chocolate or vanilla, take your pick,
Life's confusing, yet it can stick.
A generous dollop, a burst of cheer,
Even sprinkles can disappear.

With every lick, a moment missed,
Sugar highs and playful twists.
Craving sunshine in a cup,
We find contentment, fill it up.

So here's to swirls, both deep and light,
Embrace the sweet, and join the fight.
With ice cream smiles, we soften the blow,
Life's little lessons in every flow.

Bitter Sweetness of Life

A scoop of sadness, a scoop of glee,
Life's an ice cream, can't you see?
With every bite a flavor tests,
Bitter or sweet, we do our best.

A sprinkle of doubt, a chunk of fun,
Laughing through life, a race we run.
The cone might crumble, the ice cream drip,
But you can always take another trip.

Sometimes it's rocky road, so thick,
Yet every flavor has its trick.
Bitter chocolate makes us wise,
While vanilla laughs, and lightly flies.

So savor the mix, taste every hue,
For bittersweet moments help us accrue.
With joy and silliness, never end strife,
Ice cream teaches the sweet side of life.

Frosty Lessons on a Summer Day

When the sun beats down with glee,
A scoop of joy is the best remedy.
Chocolate drips and sprinkles fly,
Wipe your hands, just give a try.

Chasing cones that slip and slide,
Sometimes, you just can't take that ride.
Life's just like the melting treat,
Enjoy it fast, won't taste so sweet.

Sticky fingers and goofy grins,
Lessons learned from melting sins.
With every lick, a story's told,
Embrace the mess, let laughter unfold.

So grab a cone, don't think of fate,
Chill with the thrill, it's never too late.
When the ice cream truck comes near,
Just let your heart lead, and don't you fear.

Sweet Treats of Time

Each flavor whispers tales of old,
Of summer nights, and hearts so bold.
A scoop of courage, a pinch of fun,
Savor the day 'til the setting sun.

Sprayed in laughter, vanilla dreams,
Every choice is sweeter than it seems.
Don't fret the sprinkles that get away,
They'll find their way, come what may.

Creamy moments, like clouds of cream,
Feed your spirit, fulfill your dream.
Twists and turns like swirls of ice,
Every bite, just think twice.

So raise your cone to days gone past,
The best of flavors will forever last.
In the grand parade of treats so fine,
Every scoop is a genuine sign.

The Whirl of Surprises

Round and round, a cone on the go,
Chocolate chaos, a glorious show.
With every swirl, surprises await,
Delectable joy, it's all first-rate.

Flavors collide like minds on a spree,
Maybe bubblegum, or minty brie?
Take a chance, don't hold back dread,
You never know what's waiting ahead.

A brain freeze may come with delight,
But laughter outlasts the chilly bite.
Life, like ice cream, is best when shared,
Scoop it up, be audacious and dared.

So lean in closer, taste every thrill,
Find the sweetness—it's never too still.
With a twist and a turn, let joy become,
The frosty wonder that makes us one.

Licking the Past Away

Each lick wipes memories of yesterday,
Chocolate stains on a sunny display.
Don't fret the past, it's just a scoop,
Life's a party, let's join the troop.

Dripping joys, like times that slide,
In every flavor, let laughter abide.
Sprinkled moments, both bitter and sweet,
Savor them whole, it's never a defeat.

Every cone tells a tale of bliss,
Missed chances wrapped in creamy kiss.
So tip your hat and let it flow,
Taste the present while letting go.

With every bite, we find our way,
Fun awaits in the churn of play.
So grab a scoop, let memories sway,
Lick the past and enjoy today!

Lessons in Every Flavor

In a line for ice cream, it's clear,
A cone can bring laughter and cheer.
Strawberry's sweet, while chocolate's bold,
But do we ever taste before we're sold?

A sprinkle debate, oh what a sight,
Should I go big or keep it light?
Mint is fresh, but cookie dough's neat,
Choose wisely, my friend, it's a tasty feat.

Sticky fingers, a sugar spree,
One bite and you'll feel carefree.
Brain freeze hits, but don't despair,
Just laugh it off and breathe the air.

When cones drop, don't fret, just sigh,
Dust off your dreams, give them a try.
Taste life's flavors, no need to pout,
Every scoop gives a reason to shout!

The Sweetness of Sharing

An ice cream cart rolls down the street,
Glimmering treats make our hearts skip a beat.
A friend stands by, eyes big as the sun,
And suddenly sharing looks like so much fun.

I hand them my scoop of salted caramel,
They grin wide, oh what a swell!
A delicious bond forms with each bite,
Together we savor, everything feels right.

But what happens when flavors collide?
They want my sprinkles, but I won't hide.
With a wink and a laugh, we trade a cone,
A sprinkle of joy, we never feel alone.

We laugh as we taste life's many layers,
Sharing our cones, we become true players.
In this moment, beneath the blue sky,
It's clear: sweet friendship is worth every try!

Chill and Reflect

Alone by the cart, it's just me and ice,
I ponder decisions, and think twice.
Licking my cone as the sun starts to set,
In this quiet moment, I won't forget.

Banana split dreams, all piled up high,
Chillin' in the warmth, with a little pie.
Life's like a scoop, sometimes it's messy,
But just like ice cream, it can feel so blessy.

I watch kids run, cones held up tight,
Their giggles and shouts, pure delight.
With a crunchy sugar cone in hand,
I remember that joy is always so grand.

So sip from the milkshake, let life flow,
Embrace every dribble, let your heart glow.
Under the stars with a treat so cold,
Reflect on the moments, let your soul unfold!

Dreams Served Cold

A cart pulls near, dreams drizzled with sprinkles,
Scoop up your wishes, where laughter crinkles.
With every flavor, a story unfolds,
Each bite a promise, a treasure to hold.

Cup or cone? Oh, what a choice,
In every bite, you'll hear a voice.
Choco-chip whispers, vanilla's song,
Savor each moment, you can't go wrong.

But here's the twist that life may show,
Even melted dreams can continue to flow.
A puddle of hope left on the ground,
Find beauty in chaos, joy can be found.

So dream big, scoop deep, and take a chance,
For in every cone, there's a silly dance.
Laughter and sprinkles, oh what a sight,
Serve up your dreams, it's all pure delight!

The Cart of Choices

Beneath the sun, a cart does gleam,
A rainbow of flavors, it's like a dream.
Each scoop a choice, a swirl of fate,
Pick wisely now, don't be late!

Chocolate or strawberry, what will it be?
One scoop or two, let's wait and see.
Taste buds dancing, my heart in a spin,
Oh, the joy when you finally dig in!

When you pick a flavor, it's never just bland,
Life's like an ice cream, it's all in your hand.
Sprinkles and toppings, add some delight,
Mix it up, dear friend, make a cone that's bright!

A melting moment, gooey and sweet,
Don't rush the savor, it's quite a treat.
Embrace the chaos, the drips and the drops,
For laughter and joy, it never stops!

Savoring Each Moment

A cone in my hand, oh what a sight,
The sun on my face feels just right.
Each lick of vanilla, each bite of fudge,
Reminds me to pause; oh let's not budge!

The ice cream drips, a messy affair,
But laughter erupts; I haven't a care.
For every splash of chocolate, I beam,
Life's little moments are sweeter than cream.

Sprinkle some joy on a day that is bland,
Build castles of cones in a sugary land.
A scoop of today, a dollop of now,
Let's scoop up the fun, we'll figure out how!

So grab a spoon, we'll share in delight,
Taste buds dancing under moonlight.
For in every moment, the joy we derive,
Makes the mundane a reason to thrive!

Fudgesicles of Fortitude

Whip out a fudgesicle, cold and divine,
Frigid delight on a hot summer's line.
Each nibble brings courage, a giggle or two,
In sticky situations, it helps to chew!

Frozen treats help with worries that plague,
Fear melts away with each chocolaty swage.
Life's little troubles, they seem far away,
As I lick my popsicle; oh, let's play!

With each creamy bite, I gather my cheer,
Fudgesicles teach that joy is right here.
When life gets too serious, I simply say,
Let's chill with dessert; it's a brighter way.

So here's to the moments we savor with glee,
The world turns sweeter with a frosty decree.
Fudgesicle fortitude helps us get by,
With laughter and sweetness, we'll always fly high!

Ice Cream and Introspection

Sitting with ice cream, thoughts start to flow,
Vanilla or caramel? I ponder it slow.
Each bite ignites memories, both joyous and wild,
Like a child in a playground, I'm once again smiled.

A scoop full of laughter, a sprinkle of sorrow,
Reflections are sweet, they brighten tomorrow.
Chocolate or mint chip, I ponder with flair,
Life's just like scoops, it's better to share!

In flavors I find my introspective muse,
Mixed feelings come gentle, with flavors to choose.
From wistful to joyful, as I savor the calm,
Each lick's a reminder: I'm wrapped in a balm.

So here's to the cone and the thoughts that they bring,
With each icy scoop comes a new kind of fling.
Ice cream and wisdom, what a delightful pair,
In search of deep truths, I find they are rare!

Stories Beneath the Scoop

In a bustling street, a cart rolls by,
With a clang and a cheer, it catches the eye.
A scoop of chocolate, a swirl of glee,
Just don't ask for sprinkles—those cost a fee!

Old Mr. Whippy, he knows his trade,
With every scoop, a friendship made.
He tells the tales of cones gone wrong,
Of melting moments and flavors strong.

A child once cried, 'It slipped from my hand!'
The cone a casualty, oh, it was grand.
Mr. Whippy chuckled, as he handed a new,
Saying 'Life's just like ice cream, it's messy too!'

So next time you're faced with a sticky fate,
Remember that cart; don't think it's too late.
Scoop up the laughter, let worries slide,
For in that sweet moment, joy takes a ride.

Licking the Edge of Knowledge

With a scoop in hand, stay curious and bold,
Chasing that flavor, let the stories unfold.
Vanilla or strawberry, whatever you choose,
Knowledge drips sweetly, so don't be a snooze.

The pickle-flavored bowl, oh what a fright!
A taste of the odd, it's a pure delight.
Sometimes the weird turns the frown upside down,
Embrace all the flavors that float through the town.

While sharing a cone, a wise kid once said,
"Kindness like ice cream, is best when spread."
So share that big scoop with someone near,
There's joy in the mess; let's give a big cheer!

As toppings collide, sweet and salty collide,
Life's playful moments hide just inside.
So lick each scoop clean, don't leave it alone,
For knowledge is sweeter when shared with your own.

Cone-Dipped Realities

Under the sun, our cones wobble high,
Twirling in circles like birds in the sky.
And when the first drip starts to fall,
We laugh at the mess, it's a sticky free-for-all.

The flavors of life, both bitter and sweet,
Dance in the bowl, they make us complete.
With every crunch of the chocolate chip,
We savor the moment—don't let it slip.

A seagull swoops down, a daring thief,
Stealing my cone brings me comic grief.
Yet, in every theft, there's a lesson to find,
In laughter and chaos, we build a new mind.

So when life gets tricky and melts in the sun,
Just grab another scoop, remember the fun.
With sprinkles of laughter, and rivers of cream,
We carve our own path, chasing every dream.

Frosted Insights

In the heart of summer, the cart rolls along,
A chorus of giggles, a sweet little song.
Mint chocolate chip whispers, 'Take a big bite!'
And yet here we are, drinking root beer at night.

A spoonful of knowledge, a dash of delight,
Crammed into cones shaped by whimsy and light.
The waffle cone's crumbles, oh what a treat,
But don't drop the scoop; it's a confection defeat!

The flavors we savor, they teach us to play,
Embrace each mishap that comes our way.
For every big scoop that we fondly devour,
Is a moment that blooms, a laughter-filled hour.

So next time you're faced with a sticky dilemma,
Think of that cart—it's no crazy enigma.
With sprinkles of wisdom and drizzles of fun,
Embrace all the frosted insights, one by one.

Frozen Footprints

In summer's heat, we chase delight,
An ice cream cart comes into sight.
We giggle loud, our cones held high,
But melting dreams just trickle by.

With sticky hands and laughter bright,
We learn the joy of pure delight.
But oh, the mess, it's all around,
Like life, we stumble on this ground.

Each scoop a chance, we take a bite,
In colors bold, the world feels right.
A taste of joy, a sprinkle of fun,
In chaos sweet, we all are one.

So let the drips fall where they may,
We'll laugh and dance, come what may.
For footprints frozen in the sun,
Are silly tales for everyone!

The Art of Tasting Reality

A cone in hand, we spin in glee,
Indulging in sweet fantasy.
With every flavor, hopes align,
But every bite is not divine.

Bubblegum dreams with a sour twist,
Chocolate swirls that can't be missed.
Sometimes we find, with each new taste,
Life's sweeter things are not a waste.

In sprinkles bright, we seek the truth,
Like childhood days, we chase our youth.
So scoop it up, don't hesitate,
Embrace the good that comes your fate.

A scoop arrives with laughter loud,
Together eating in a crowd.
Reality's bittersweet and grand,
So savor it, just like you planned!

Whirlwinds of Change

The ice cream truck rolls down the street,
A symphony of laughs and heat.
We gather round, our hearts a-flutter,
As flavors mix, oh what a clutter!

The twists and turns of every scoop,
Mirror life's unpredictable loop.
Some days we taste the salty tears,
Then scoop up joy to calm our fears.

With rainbow swirls and sprightly cheer,
Change tastes sweet throughout the year.
A melted cone can teach us all,
To rise and shine, despite the fall.

So take a bite of life's parade,
With every lick, a memory made.
In whirlwinds of flavors, we find grace,
A scoop of joy in every place!

Confectionery Chronicles

In ice cream lore, we find our voice,
With every scoop, we make a choice.
Fudge cascades, a story flows,
Among the cones, our laughter grows.

We stumble upon flavors odd,
Beetroot cream? A tiny nod!
Crunchy bits and gooey swirls,
Unfamiliar tastes, they dance and twirl.

We learn to share, to scoop and serve,
The sweetest lessons we preserve.
For in each cone, there lies a tale,
Of friendships forged, and dreams set sail.

So gather round the cart today,
Where smiles have their playful way.
With every bite, our stories stick,
A confectionery magic, thick!

The Art of Balancing Flavors

In the cart, a swirl of treats,
A scoop of giggles, life repeats.
Chocolate, vanilla, mixed delight,
Balancing sweetness, not a fright.

A scoop too big? Oh what a mess!
Drips and slips, who would guess?
Cones tilted high, a sticky show,
Laughter's the flavor we all know.

Choices abound, a playful game,
Want it all? Don't feel the shame!
Life's like sprinkles, colored bright,
It's all about that fun-filled bite.

So laugh and scoop, lay worries low,
Each flavor tells tales, let them flow.
With every taste, a lesson sweet,
Find joy in chaos, life's fun treat.

Beneath the Cherry Top

Beneath the cherry, dreams reside,
A burst of joy, let's have a ride.
Each topping tells a quirky tale,
Of melting moments, never stale.

Whipped cream clouds, a frothy dance,
In sticky hands, we take a chance.
Life's too short for just plain fries,
Indulge in sweetness, oh, how it flies!

The sprinkles spark like stars at night,
In errant laughter, we find our light.
With every lick, the world's less grim,
Under that cherry, we learn to swim.

So grab your cone, let's chase the sun,
Each bite a giggle, just pure fun.
In cherry tops, our dreams align,
Let's savor joy, one scoop at a time.

Reflections in a Delicate Dish

A bowl of joy, reflections shine,
Scoops piled high and oh, so fine.
Life served up in colors bright,
Each spoonful giggles, pure delight.

Dishes swirl like stories told,
In creamy shapes, adventure bold.
Strawberries dip, adventures blend,
Each taste a twist, a happy trend.

A little spoon, a crunchy bite,
Life's happiness, pure and light.
So let's devour, dash of cream,
In this sweet dish, we craft our dream.

With every scoop, let worries flee,
Embrace the silly, wild, and free.
Reflections melt and laughter swishes,
Serve up the joy in every dish.

The Colors of Every Season

Summer shines with lemon zest,
Winter's chill, hot fudge is best.
Autumn arrives with pumpkin cheer,
Spring's fresh mint, clap your hands here!

Scoops like seasons, swirling fast,
Moments melt; they never last.
With every taste, a season sings,
In buttery cones, happiness clings.

Taste the rainbow, flavors play,
Life's an ice cream, bright display.
Cherry blossoms lift the mood,
Every waffle cone, a gratitude.

So grab your friends, a double scoop,
Celebrate each quirky loop.
In every season, one thing's true,
With every bite, we start anew.

Sweet Whispers in the Frost

In summer's blaze, a cart rolls by,
Chasing dreams with a cheerful sigh.
Flavors dance in a rainbow swirl,
Each scoop a tale, each cone a twirl.

Laughter mingles with sticky hands,
As sprinkles fall like golden sands.
The more you share, the more you gain,
A scoop of joy, a dash of pain.

With every lick, the worries fade,
Chocolate dreams in the sun's parade.
Frosty bites of sweet delight,
Remind us all to hold on tight.

So let us feast on creamy bliss,
Each moment savored, not to miss.
The funny truth, as bold as cream,
Is life's a scoop, a funny dream.

The Flavor of Resilience

A cone falls down, oh what a sight,
The rainbow drips in perfect flight.
We laugh it off, what's done is done,
There's always more; let's have some fun!

When mint chip mocks the sunny day,
We scoop another; that's the way.
Life's not just vanilla, plain and sweet,
It's a rocky road, a wild treat.

So dig in deep, face the unknown,
With every swirl, you've brightly grown.
A sprinkle of grit, a dash of flair,
Helps make the best flavors to share!

With every scoop, a lesson dear,
That flavors blossom through the fear.
So grab a spoon, let's fill our cup,
In this sweet ride, we'll never give up.

Melting Moments of Clarity

Under the sun, we chase delight,
Ice cream smiles, a pure insight.
As cones grow soggy, drop and slide,
We learn to savor, not to hide.

Two scoops top, a mountain high,
But watch it melt, oh me, oh my!
In drips and drops, the truth appears,
Life's fleeting joys are worth the cheers.

We chase the cart, we run, we shout,
In every stumble, there's no doubt.
A brain freeze comes, then fades away,
Teaching us to laugh, to play.

So cherish each frosty, fleeting taste,
In melted moments, don't let haste.
Let's lick the day, both wild and true,
For every scoop brings a laugh anew.

Scoops of Wisdom

A scoop of humor, a sprinkle of fun,
Life's better shared, and never done.
With flavors bold and colors bright,
A frosty treat in the warm sunlight.

When caramel drips, we stand and cheer,
And with each cone, we shift the gear.
Lessons serve in unexpected ways,
Like melted ice cream on hot days.

So when the cart rolls into view,
Take a moment, taste the brew.
For wisdom's served in every bite,
In laughter's cone, we find our light.

Keep scooping high, don't hesitate,
In this sweet life, it's never too late.
For every flavor, a path unfolds,
A story told as the ice cream molds.

Whirling Cream Dreams

In a world of sprinkles and delight,
Choices loom in colors bright.
Every scoop holds a tale,
Waffle cones never fail.

Choco chips in a swirl,
It's a sweet, chaotic whirl.
Don't fret if it tips and spills,
Just laugh; that's how life fulfills.

What if the flavors start to blend?
Sometimes chaos is a friend.
Peanut butter and mint collide,
In this mess, take pride!

So grab your cone, let's have some fun,
Life's a sundae, never done.
Just a lick, and you might see,
Ridiculous joy is key!

Epiphanies in a Soft Serve

A twist of fate on a sunny day,
Soft serve dreams in a creamy way.
Chocolate or vanilla, what's your pick?
Decisions melt—oh so quick!

One scoop's worth can surprise the soul,
The drips and drops make you feel whole.
Embrace the flops, the gooey mess,
In life's kitchen, it's all a guess!

When sprinkles fall like confetti rare,
You realize joy is everywhere.
A cherry on top, what a view!
It's the little things that get you through.

So swirl your way through the twisty cone,
Laugh at the ice that's overblown.
Frosting wisdom in every bite,
Let's sing praises of sugary delight!

A Journey in Every Scoop

With every scoop, a story starts,
Different flavors, different hearts.
A journey made with each cone held,
Unexpected treats may be dispelled.

A sprinkle here, a fudge layer there,
Navigating life with a goofy flair.
What's the point of a perfect cone?
Enjoy the crumbles, you're never alone!

Tasting life with a giggle and grin,
Let the wild toppings begin!
Raspberry ripple, lemon zest,
Every ingredient's a funny quest.

So here's to the drips and spills we face,
Like melted ice cream in its race.
Savor the moments, and don't forget,
Every journey's a scoop you won't regret!

Cones of Experience

Cone in hand, the sun on high,
Twists of wisdom make you fly.
Chocolate fudge, sticky and sweet,
In this mess, we find our beat.

Tasting flavors, wild and new,
Every bite a clue or two.
Like caramel spills that grace the floor,
Life's all about exploring more!

What if the cone is cracked just right?
Embrace the chaos; hold on tight!
When life gives you sprinkles, be bold,
A crunchy story waiting to be told.

As you navigate this frosty land,
Make silly faces—be unplanned.
For every scoop offers a chance,
To giggle, savor, and dance!

Frosty Adventures

On the corner, it stands bright,
Waving dreams in pastel light.
Scoops of joy, oh what a sight,
Chasing frowns with pure delight.

A sprightly bell rings loud and clear,
Sugar cones bring grins and cheer.
Sprinkled laughter, we hold dear,
In every scoop, there's warmth near.

You think you want a triple stack,
But one tiny scoop is no whack!
We all find out, and that's the knack,
Just wear your joy, and never lack.

So let's indulge in silly games,
In the cart, we forget our names.
Life's a swirl of fruity flames,
With laughter sprinkled like love's claims.

Creamy Contemplations

Beneath the sun, we gather round,
An ice cream cart, magic found.
With every flavor, joy is crowned,
In melted dreams, our hearts unbound.

The minty swirl makes shadows dance,
While chocolate chips leave little chance.
With every scoop, we take a glance,
At sprinkles adding to the romance.

We ponder life in waffle bowls,
Contemplating soft-serve roles.
Is it better to blend or stroll?
Or just embrace the yummy tolls?

So grab a spoon, do not despair,
In every cone, find joy to share.
Silly moments fill the air,
With creamy smiles, why not dare?

The Twist of Fate

A twist of fate in every scoop,
Like spinning tales in a goofball troop.
Who knew sprinkles could make us stoop,
While laughter erupts in one big whoop?

Sundae toppings piled on high,
A cherry tiptoes like it can fly.
With whipped cream hats, we're that silly guy,
And in this carnival, we can defy.

What happens next is any guess,
The cone may wobble, but we won't stress.
With each sweet bite, we still profess,
In this frosty world, we're all a mess.

So when in doubt, just order more,
Life's a journey with an open door.
In every scoop, let spirits soar,
With flavors that we all adore.

Sundae Secrets

Underneath the candy peaks,
Lie secrets sweet as summer weeks.
In every scoop, the silly speaks,
As laughter hides in creamy streaks.

A cherry plopped with such a flair,
Whipped cream, dancing in the air.
We mix our troubles, unaware,
With sticky fingers, life's a dare.

The sprinkles wink from higher ground,
While neighbors smile as joy is found.
In these small moments, laughter bound,
Sundaes become our sacred ground.

So when life serves a rocky road,
Shift gears, lighten up the load.
With every cone, share laughter's ode,
In every scoop, sweet joy bestowed.

Frozen Journeys

Under the sun, with a cart so bright,
Little ones giggle, what a sight!
Chasing dreams in a cone so grand,
Each scoop a treasure, life's sweet brand.

Sticky fingers and laughter loud,
Sharing flavors, we feel so proud.
Chocolate drips and sprinkles fly,
With every lick, we learn to try.

Melting moments, oh what a race,
In sticky mess, we find our place.
When spritz of joy begins to fade,
We nab another, not afraid!

So let's enjoy this frosty spree,
For in this cart, we're wild and free.
Each scoop a lesson, a silly cheer,
Life's a cone, so grab it, dear!

The Cart That Carries Memories

Rolling down the street with flair,
That wheeled delight, a breath of air.
Each flavor tells a tale we know,
Of summers past and laughter's glow.

Sticky hands and melting dreams,
A dash of giggles, or so it seems.
Vanilla whispers stories sweet,
While bubblegum will dance on feet.

Sundae splashes, oh what a mess,
Toppings falling, such happiness!
With every bite, we'll reminisce,
In flavors found, pure childhood bliss.

With a swirl of joy and sprinkles bright,
This cart brings memories to the light.
Here's a scoop for the tales that stay,
Each lick a giggle, come what may!

Flavors of Familiarity

Minty freshness, a zing of zest,
Chocolate fudge, among the best.
Each flavor brings a friend's embrace,
In this cart, we find our place.

Cotton candy clouds, a sugar rush,
Memories swirl in a playful hush.
Tasting joy, with every bite,
In every cone, a laugh ignites.

Strawberry smiles and lemon highs,
As pop songs play, our spirits rise.
We sip the sun, with laughter loud,
Together we dance, a silly crowd.

With every scoop, we gather round,
In every sweet taste, friendship found.
So savor the laughs, and take a chance,
In flavors of life, we twirl and dance!

Scoop by Scoop

Two scoops of fun, one scoop of cheer,
Wobbly cones, but who would fear?
Chocolate chip dreams like big fluffy clouds,
Beneath the sun, we laugh and shout.

Jumbling flavors in silly ways,
Each frozen treat, a giggly praise.
Caramel drips from pie-eyed grins,
With a dash of chaos, the fun begins.

Popsicles freeze, but hearts stay warm,
In every dip, a memory's charm.
Scoop by scoop, we learn to play,
In the sweetest madness, we find our way.

So roll with the carts, let laughter soar,
In every bite, we'll crave for more.
Together we revel, oh what a scene,
In this frosty dance, we reign like kings!

www.ingramcontent.com/pod-product-compliance
Lightning Source LLC
Chambersburg PA
CBHW051643160426
43209CB00004B/770